Conversation Starters

for

Anderson Cooper's

The Rainbow Comes and Goes

By dailyBooks

FREE Download: Bonus Books Included
*Claim Yours with **Any Purchase** of* Conversation Starters!

How to claim your free download:

1.   LEAVE MY AMAZON REVIEW.

You Can Also Use the "Write a Customer Review" Button

2.   ENTER YOUR BEST EMAIL HERE.

NO SPAM. Your Email is Never Shared and is Protected

Or Scan QR Code

3.   RECEIVE YOUR FREE DOWNLOAD.

Download is Delivered Instantly to Inbox

Please Note: This is an unofficial conversation starters guide. If you have not yet read the original work, please do so first.

We hope you enjoy this complementary guide from **dailyBooks**. *We aim to provide quality, thought provoking material to assist in your discovery and discussions on some of today's favorite books.*

Tips for Using dailyBooks Conversation Starters:

EVERY GOOD BOOK CONTAINS A WORLD FAR DEEPER THAN the surface of its pages. The characters and their world come alive through the words on the pages, yet the characters and its world still live on. Questions herein are designed to bring us beneath the surface of the page and invite us into the world that lives on. These questions can be used to:

- Foster a deeper understanding of the book
- Promote an atmosphere of discussion for groups
- Assist in the study of the book, either individually or corporately
- Explore unseen realms of the book as never seen before

About Us:

THROUGH YEARS OF EXPERIENCE AND FIELD EXPERTISE, from newspaper featured book clubs to local library chapters, *dailyBooks* can bring your book discussion to life. Host your book party as we discuss some of today's most widely read books.

Table of Contents

Introducing *The Rainbow Comes and Goes*

THE RAINBOW COMES AND GOES BY ANDERSON COOPER and Gloria Vanderbilt is a book summing the year-long email conversations between the writers, mother and son, about their lives, including details of love and loss. It starts at the beginning of 2015, around the time of Gloria Vanderbilt's ninety-first birthday, after she is hospitalized with a respiratory infection. The book was inspired by an idea of Anderson Cooper's— whether he and his mother were actually as close and intimate as they thought or could be. These original thoughts lead him to the fact that he barely knew about his mother's past, when compared to that of his late father's. He wanted to learn from her, from her experiences and the life lessons she wanted to pass down herself, neither of which he had ever asked her about. Thus, this book is set forth in the hope of inspiring its readers to start a long-due conversation with their loved ones—one that would help them learn and improve their relationships.

The book includes illustrations and some interesting quotes, but is mostly conversations covered in extreme detail—it seems to the reader almost as if the authors' are reliving their lives in front of the audience's eyes. They start telling each other their experiences, and what their lives were like, starting from their childhood to the present. The book takes its readers through various times (1925 – 2015), cities (New York City, Los Angeles), and countries (US, France, UK) with major celebrities. It gives a sneak peek into the lives of celebrities as narrated by the celebrities themselves. Although the details are extremely personal and intimate—involving details about families, love life, sex, loss, etc., it is elegantly composed. All the conversations ultimately show each of the authors' love and respect for each other because they never had a chance to express it previously.

Thus, the book encourages its readers to take the first step towards getting to know their loved ones—if they haven't done so already—and shows them a glimpse of what their lives could be like—all the better.

Introducing the Author

ANDERSON HAYS COOPER, 49, BORN IN NEW YORK CITY IS the youngest son of late writer, Wyatt Cooper. He studied and graduated early from a renowned private school in New York City, Dalton School. He then attended Trumbull College at Yale University and graduated with a Bachelor of Arts in Political Science. During a stay in Vietnam, he also attended the University of Hanoi and studied the native language. He began working as a fact checker at Channel One, a digital media and content provider, prior to beginning his career in journalism. After several trials, he finally became a reporter for the same company. He joined ABC News as a correspondent and then became a co-anchor for the famous overnight program, World News Now. After a quick detour working for a reality show, he started working for CNN with his now famous show, Anderson Cooper 360° and Anderson Live. Apart from being a journalist, he is also a freelance writer of non-fiction, including works of memories and books from personal experiences, mostly about loss.

Gloria Laura Vanderbilt, 92, was also born in New York City into a millionaire family, to Reginald Claypoole Vanderbilt and Gloria Morgan. As an infant, she lost her father and became an heiress to a fund of $10 million, sharing half of it with her sister. Growing up, she attended various schools across the northeast. Later she attended Arts Students League in New York City, getting a background for the career ahead of her. Needless to say, she became an actress working in theater arts, followed by reality and recorded shows in the television industry. Apart from being a famous actress, she is also a fashion designer with a line of jeans, linen, scarves, etc. She is also known for her artwork using pastels, watercolors, and oils. Last, but not least, she, like her son is also an author of various memoirs and novels.

Discussion Questions

. . . .

question 1

The author says she was scared of her mother even as a youth.
Discuss what it might feel like to be afraid of a parent? What
might be the reasons for that?

. . . .

. . . .

question 2

Referring to the statement above, did you/do you fear your
parent/a significant person in your family and why?

. . . .

question 3

Anderson Cooper's mother, Gloria Vanderbilt didn't have much interaction or closeness with her mother or her father. In the book, Anderson Cooper says that he could always feel his mother's discomfort in that role. Do you think people who haven't had much interaction with their parents during childhood feel inadequate to become parents themselves? Discuss why/why not.

. . . .

question 4

Gloria Vanderbilt says that she considers her mother to be a magical stranger for her. Discuss the possible qualities of such a personality in terms of a parent.

. . . .

question 5

Referring to above, how/what phrase(s) would you use to
describe Ms. Vanderbilt's mother and why?

question 6

Gloria Vanderbilt references some terrible thoughts she used to have as a kid because of the lack of intimacy with her mother. Discuss the possible thoughts of a kid who doesn't have an intimate relationship with his/her mother.

question 7

Gloria Vanderbilt says that when she was 10, she started living with her aunt, who barely knew her until then. Discuss the possible positive and negative aspects that each of them would've had to face in that circumstance on a daily basis.

. . . .

question 8

When she was a kid, Gloria Vanderbilt's mother and aunt fought for her custody. Finally, her aunt won the trial. Discuss how it might've felt for Gloria to leave her mother permanently and live with her aunt.

. . . .

. . . .

question 9

Referring to the statement above, does your opinion change after
learning the fact that Gloria herself might have wanted to live
with her aunt rather than her mother?

. . . .

. . . .

question 10

According to the author, homosexuality was considered a crime.
Do you know of anyone from your family who was homosexual
during those times? How do their lives and struggles compare to
those of today?

. . . .

. . . .

question 11

Gloria Vanderbilt says in one of her responses to Anderson
Cooper that according to her, those who are gay/lesbian are
lucky. Why do you think she said that?

. . . .

. . . .

question 12

Referring to the above statement, do you see yourself relating to
it—do you feel that LGBT have an advantage over heterosexual
individuals/couples? Why or why not?

. . . .

. . . .

question 13

For Gloria Vanderbilt, success came when she knew she had
pleased others to a satisfactory extent. Did you ever see yourself
or know anyone in such a circumstance? How did you/they get
yourself/themselves out of it?

. . . .

. . . .

question 14

Both the authors of the book agree that it is always better to bury the past and move forward and to always make that a priority. What could be some of the disadvantages of doing so?

. . . .

. . . .

question 15

At the beginning of the book, Anderson Cooper said that growing up, the conversations between his mother and him decreased significantly. Was this the case in your family as well? Did the conversations between you and your parents decrease? What do you think happens in general, and why is that the case?

. . . .

. . . .

question 16

The book gives certain expectations to its readers prior to reading it. Does the book live up to the expectations you had prior to reading it? Why or why not?

. . . .

· ·

question 17

The book is entitled *The Rainbow Comes and Goes*. Why do you
think the authors chose this title?

· ·

. . . .

question 18

While reviewing the book, a Bay area reporter said that this book is the ideal gift for Mother's day or even Father's day. Do you agree? Why or why not?

. . . .

. . . .

question 19

Referring to the statement above, why do you think this book is considered to be one of the best gifts for Mother's day or Father's day?

. . . .

question 20

Andy Cohen said that the book will speak to all mothers and sons of all generations. Do you agree? Why or why not?

FREE Download: Bonus Books Included

*Claim Yours with **Any Purchase** of Conversation Starters!*

How to claim your free download:

4.   LEAVE MY AMAZON REVIEW.
You Can Also Use "Write a Customer Review" Button

5.   ENTER YOUR BEST EMAIL HERE.
NO SPAM. Your Email is Never Shared and is Protected

Or Scan Above

6.   RECEIVE YOUR FREE DOWNLOAD.
Download is Instantly Delivered to Inbox

question 21

In their review, the *New York Times* said that the book was remarkably frank. Do you think the frankness in the conversations was necessary? Why or why not?

. . . .

question 22

The book is basically an exchange of email conversations
between its writers. Is there any conversation that is particularly
memorable for you?

. . . .

question 23

Many movie directors like to take a book as their inspiration in making a movie. Do you think this book would make a good movie? Would it have the same kind of impression on its audience as its readers? Why or why not?

. . . .

question 24

The book's purpose is to inspire its readers and encourage them
to speak to their loved ones in order to live a better life. Do you
think the book lived up to its purpose? Why or why not?

. . . .

question 25

Andy Cohen thought some of the events mentioned in the book were funny. Was there any conversation that was particularly funny for you? Describe the conversation and explain why you found it particularly funny.

. . . .

question 26

Both the authors of the book agree that it is always better to bury the past and move forward and always make that a priority. Do you agree/disagree with the authors? Why or why not?

. . . .

. . . .

question 27

For Gloria Vanderbilt, success came when she knew she had pleased others to a satisfactory extent. Discuss the confidence and self-respect a person like Gloria exudes.

. . . .

. . . .

question 28

Gloria Vanderbilt says she used to fantasize and hope that death wouldn't happen to her. If you were her, would you hope for the same? Why or why not?

. . . .

. . . .

question 29

According to Ms. Vanderbilt, good health is a boon, one that is to be treasured. What do you consider to be your treasured gift for life and why?

. . . .

. . . .

question 30

Both the authors hope that the conversations between them will help motivate their readers to bridge the gap between their loved ones and themselves. Do you think this book would be able to do that for generations to come? Why or why not?

. . . .

question 31

If you were to give an example of a conventional mother-son relationship, who would you exemplify and why?

question 32

The author says that in order to bring a positive change in a relationship, honesty is a must. If you were the author of this book, which key attribute/personality change would you recommend to your readers for bringing a positive change in a relationship and why?

. . . .

. . . .

question 33

Anderson Cooper compares himself to a shark, an animal that always has to move forward in order to live. What would you compare yourself to and why?

. . . .

· ·

question 34

For Gloria Vanderbilt, success came when she knew she had pleased others to a satisfactory extent. If you were in her situation, what would you consider your success?

· ·

. . . .

question 35

As a kid, Gloria Vanderbilt's mother and aunt fought for her custody. Finally, her aunt won custody. If the same were to happen today, how do you think the circumstances would be different?

. . . .

. . . .

question 36

Gloria Vanderbilt references some terrible thoughts she used to
have as a kid because of the lack of intimacy with her mother.
Imagine yourself as Gloria Vanderbilt. What kind of
nightmares/thoughts would you have experienced as a result of
lack of intimacy with your mother?

. . . .

. . . .

question 37

The author says that she wasn't much of an expressive person and that the elderly didn't talk much to the young. If these were the situations in the current times, especially in your family, describe its impact on the kids in your family.

. . . .

· ·

question 38

If you were the author of this book, what would you have named
it and why?

· ·

Quiz Questions

. . . .

question 39

Gloria Vanderbilt used to call her nanny ------.

. . . .

question 40

True or false: Gloria Vanderbilt was very close to her mother.

question 41

True or false: Gloria Vanderbilt was an only child.

question 42

True or false: Both Gloria Vanderbilt and Anderson Cooper lost their fathers when they were reasonably young.

question 43

True or false: The trial for custody of Gloria Vanderbilt was won by her mother.

question 44

True or false: The conversations in the book are mostly funny.

question 45

True or false: Anderson Cooper sees himself as one with the qualities of a shark.

question 46

True or false: According to Gloria Vanderbilt, being born into a millionaire family is a boon, one that is to be treasured.

question 47

Gloria Vanderbilt says ------------ is a boon.

question 48

True or false: Anderson Cooper spent a year in Vietnam.

question 49

True or false: Anderson Cooper is a freelance writer.

question 50

True or false: Ever since his childhood, Anderson Cooper knew his mother and her past very well.

Quiz Answers

1. Dodo
2. False; in the first few chapters of the book, she describes that she didn't have an intimate relationship with her mother.
3. False; she had a sister.
4. True
5. False; her aunt won the trial.
6. False; they are sometimes funny but mostly serious real-life experiences.
7. True
8. False; she considered good health to be a boon.
9. good health
10. True
11. True
12. False; growing up, the conversations he had with his mother decreased significantly.

THE END

Want to promote your book group?
Register here.

FREE Download: Bonus Books Included
*Claim Yours with **Any Purchase** of Conversation Starters!*

How to claim your free download:

7.   LEAVE MY AMAZON REVIEW.
You Can Also Use "Write a Customer Review" Button

8.   ENTER YOUR BEST EMAIL HERE.
NO SPAM. Your Email is Never Shared and is Protected

Or Scan Above

9.   RECEIVE YOUR FREE DOWNLOAD.
Download is Instantly Delivered to Inbox

Made in the USA
Columbia, SC
06 December 2022